6 PILLARS TO POWER UP YOUR MIND
MENTAL HEALTH IS A LIFESTYLE! ®

6 PILLARS TO POWER UP YOUR MIND

MENTAL HEALTH IS A LIFESTYLE! ®

*How to Power Up Your Mind
and Live the Life That You Desire*

I stand on the shoulders of many, including: Lorraine, Marion, Blonnie, and Shakirah.

Thank You
Ayanna, the world is yours!

by
ANDREA WISE-BROWN

M.Ed., LPC., NCC
Psychotherapist and Mental-Health Expert

ISBN 13#: 9781087075143

MENTAL
HEALTH/WELLNESS/HEALTH/LIFESTYLE/WOMEN/MEN

Library of Congress Cataloging-In-Publication Data is available from publisher.

This book is available for bulk discounts. For more information contact: www.awisebrown.com

Printed in the United States

Table of Contents

INTRODUCTION

You have the Power to co-create the life you truly desire… if you get your mind right.

Hi there! Thanks for picking up my "how to" guide to supercharging your mental health…so you can keep WINNING! In today's "boss up" culture, people are living out loud, walking in their truth, and securing the "bag" all on their way to destination "My Best Life Avenue." I too am a life traveler and encourage you to enjoy the ride! I also urge you to adopt life habits that will help you keep your mind right.

Keeping your mind right has all to do with being proactive while taking care of your brain. The average size of a brain is about 3 pounds, which represents three pounds of magic. Your brain (magic) controls your body's movement, physical functioning, logistical processing, emotional intelligence, and how you perceive all that exists in the world.

Introduction

As a mental-health expert and psychotherapist with more than 15 years of experience, I often see people who are just coming to the realization that they are mentally and emotionally exhausted. The inability to effectively deal with the pressures of life is a sign that your brain is malfunctioning. If it's failing, so are other areas that contribute to your Quality of Life, such as your finances, romantic relationships, career, familial relationships, and parenting.

Your mind (brain) is your body's engine. Just like a car's engine, you must maintain it with regular maintenance for it to perform at its best. Your brain also needs special care for it to perform at its best, so I want to provide you with six pillars that will keep your mind healthy and strong, if you put them into practice.

There are many spiritual teachers, life coaches and strategists who will sell you on all types of plans to change your life. The truth is: They may be right about what they are teaching you. However, none of it can be accomplished without doing exactly what I am going to teach you to do here first.

You must take care of your Mental Health (the mind, which include: psychological, social, and emotional wellbeing) in order to build the fruitful life that you desire. Imagine this: How silly it would be to begin to build your dream home with the roof, or a beautiful marble backsplash backing the kitchen sink, or better yet a fantastic chandelier

Introduction

in the foyer without building the foundation? For a house to be sturdy, strong, reliable, resilient, and everlasting it must have a strong, sturdy foundation which is created first before any other part of the home.

Staying proactive with building your mental health is doing the same thing: creating stability in your life. By being proactive with your mental health, you are creating resilience and strength before any of life's storms come your way.

Now let me teach you how to make Mental Health your Lifestyle so you can turn your life all the way up and live the life that you truly desire.

Pillar One :

Exercise and Mental Health

A healthy body is so much stronger with a healthy brain.

Exercise and Mental Health

A healthy body is so much stronger with a healthy brain.

The first step to making mental health a lifestyle is literally taking a step. Despite its simplicity, countless people struggle to make exercise a priority in their life. In fact, exercise is the first casualty of the high achiever's busy schedule replaced by "high-in-sugar" energy drinks, bad relationships, unhealthy eating habits, and self medication.

In the culture of plastic surgery and quick fixes, exercise still reigns supreme when it comes to inner and outer transformation. Quick fixes only offer a temporary solution.

Unfortunately, people experiencing challenges to their mental health seldom view exercise as a mental-health safeguard. Moreover, they rarely equate their lack of energy, clouded thinking, and mood swings to their aversion to physical activity. However, the psychological benefits of exercise cannot be understated.

A lifestyle of exercise raises the dopamine (feel-good) neurotransmitters in your brain as well as reduces stress, helps minimize the symptoms of depression, and boosts your brain's power. In my private practice, I encourage my clients to make exercise a key pillar in their mental-health makeover because of its many benefits.

Benefits of Exercise on the Brain

I'm not alone in my assessment. Research points to five clear advantages of adding exercise into your mental-health regimen, (Shawan, Charles)[1].

1. Exercise helps depression and anxiety.
Recent studies show that roughly 43 million Americans have a diagnosable mental disorder, (National Institute of Mental Health)[2].
Exercise is an effective tool to combating bouts of extreme sadness and fear by kicking off your endorphin levels, which serve as a natural mood enhancer.

2. Exercise helps manage stress.
"Studies show that it is very effective at reducing fatigue, improving alertness and concentration, and at enhancing overall cognitive functioning. This can be especially helpful when stress has depleted your energy or ability to concentrate" (Anxiety and Depression Association of America-ADAA)[3].

3. Exercise Improves Self Esteem and Confidence.

Exercising builds muscle, improves stamina, and increases self-love. When one feels physically fit, one feels stronger, more flexible and confident. Who doesn't want to feel strong enough to face life's challenges?

4. Exercise Improves Your Sleep.

Though it's not a good idea to exercise before you lie down for the night, having an exercise routine during the day will help you rest better. One of the many benefits of exercise is that it increases the body's temperature, which causes a calming effect on the brain. Sleep also regulates your circadian rhythm, which controls when you feel awake and alert.

5. Exercise boosts your brain.

Exercise increases the amount of grey matter in the pre-frontal lobe, which heightens your creativity and level of motivation. Exercise also aids in the brain's capability to reason more effectively and increases your decision-making ability.

An article posted on the Harvard Medical School Health Publishing blog yielded results proving that regular exercise sharpens intelligence while finding the opposite occurs for people who lead sedentary lifestyles. Lack of exercise dulled their intelligence,(Godman, Heidi 2018₄.

So if you want to be smart and keep your brain sharp, you must exercise, no more excuses! Adopting an exercise regime is the first pillar with your mental-health success.

It's never too late to get started, even if your last doctor's visit revealed you had a BMI bordering on obesity. Don't be distracted by a crowded imagination and unclear vision. Your mind is capable of making good life decisions. Get up, throw on a pair of sneakers and a pair of comfortable tights and go for a walk.

Let's Get Moving

When it comes to exercising, people's excuses for not working out run a gamut of reasons. From not having time to not having enough energy to exercise, people constantly make up reasons why they can't push themselves to be better.

The only way to defeat these excuses is to reveal and remove the barriers that are hindering your progress. The following are a few helpful tips to help you get started.

Tips to Accommodate Exercise

- Make time to exercise
  Set some time aside to integrate a little bit of exercise into your daily routine. Before you start, consult your doctor to let them know your plan to increase your physical activity. Include both high impact exercises as well as lots of stretching and time to recover.

- Select a workout you enjoy and will maintain. People work really hard at what they like to do, so I advise you to do an exercise program that you like, which will increase the likelihood for you to stick with the program,(Dregni, Michael 2019)[5].

- Set realistic goals as it relates to your workout plan. If you haven't exercised in 10 years, you want to slowly introduce progressively intense workouts. If you start out too hard, you may want to quit.

- Get an accountability partner. Including a friend to help you stay on track is a great way to help you reach your goals. Ask someone you trust to join you on a walk or for a fun dance class.

Exercises that are Good for your Mental Health

When it comes to mental health, there are a few exercises that may be more grounding than others. However, most exercises release "feel-good" hormones in your body. I've included a few exercises to help you start on your way to a mentally healthy lifestyle.

Low-Intensity Exercise (Walking, Pilates)

Research has found that low-intensity aerobic activity is the best form of exercise for encouraging positive thoughts and improving alertness.

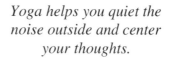

Yoga

Yoga is a form of meditation that can be soothing and calming for those suffering with anxiety or depression.

Yoga helps you quiet the noise outside and center your thoughts.

11

Swimming
Swimming allows you to clear your mind in the tranquil waters.

Cycling
Cycling increases the heart rate. This contributes to optimum brain function similar to the effects of exercise on healthy muscles.

Dance
Dance is a fun and interactive way to improve your self esteem, and practice memory skills and coordination. Your local community center should have a fun dance class for you to enroll in (Dr. Sharma, Dr. Madaan, Dr. Petty, 2019)[6].

The Wise Mind-Body Challenge

In the upcoming days, I encourage you to integrate Pillar 1, **Exercise and Mental Health** into your life. Doing so will help you develop the discipline you need to take care of your engine on a daily basis to avoid erosion or degenerative malfunctions due to lack of maintenance.

Use the following lines to journal about how you feel after you've added exercise into your daily regiment.

_____

_____

_____

_____

_____

_____

_____

_____

_____

Pillar One: Exercise and Mental Health

_____

_____

_____

_____

_____

_____

_____

_____

_____

_____

_____

_____

_____

_____

Pillar Two:
Nutrition and Mental Health

Your thinking determines whether you will fly or crawl for the rest of your life.

Nutrition and Mental Health

Your thinking determines whether you will fly or crawl for the rest of your life.

Do you know that your diet can greatly impact your mental health? Most people know eating a healthy diet can protect them from high blood pressure, obesity and heart disease. However, a new and exciting field of psychiatry called Nutritional Psychiatry is emerging, which studies reveal a healthy diet can "power up" your brain too.

Since the early 2000s, research has come to the forefront pointing to a connection between what one eats and drinks to how one feels and acts. In fact, in an article written by Columbia University's assistant clinical professor of psychiatry, Dr. Drew Ramsey, states, "Diet is potentially the most powerful intervention we have. By helping people shape their diets, we can improve their mental health, and decrease the risk of psychiatric disorders."

It's empowering to know that you can take control of your mental health by making "Neuronutrition" a priority in your life. "Neuronutrition" is intentionally packing your diet with "brain food" that supports your brain's health and heightens cognitive functioning. Simply put, if you eat right, you can think right and Pillar 2, **Feed your Brain,** is all about developing a Neuro-Nutrition Plan that helps your brain reach its optimal performance.

The Brain-Food Connection

Proof of food's impact on one's brain started to become evident as researchers began to recognize individuals who ate diets filled with Omega 3s, nuts, berries and whole grains (Harvard School of Public Health, 2019)7. Individuals using the Mediterranean and Japanese diets exhibited less symptoms of depression. The people who ate Western diets packed with refined sugar, salt and high-saturated fat experienced more symptoms of depression. Furthermore, in the journal, "Brain Behavior and Immunity," a study found an association between depression and a diet rich in sugar, sweetened soft drinks, refined grains and red meat.

Below is the Mediterranean Food Pyramid to provide a visual example of a diet filled with "brain food." You can begin to add these foods to power up your mental health.

MEDITERRANEAN FOOD PYRAMID
The Essentials to a "Healthy-Mind" Diet

MEATS AND SWEETS
(Less Often)

POULTRY, EGGS, CHEESE, AND YOGURT
(Moderate Portions, Daily to Weekly)

FISH AND SEAFOOD,
(Often, at least two times per week)

FRUITS, VEGETABLES, GRAINS (MOSTLY WHOLE), OLIVE OIL, BEANS, NUTS, LEGUMES, SEEDS, HERBS AND SPICES
(Base every meal on these foods)

GET ACTIVE
(Incorporate some type of physical exercise at least three days a week)

The Brain-Stomach Connection

What's most important for you to understand is that the entire process of fueling your brain begins in your stomach. As stated earlier, if your brain is your life's engine, then the nutrients you eat and drink are your life's fuel. In an article in "Science Digest,"the stomach is referred to as your "super highway" to the brain or as your second brain.

Moreover, the production of these "super highways" is activated when your body produces serotonin. Serotonin is a powerful neurotransmitter that controls your mood, appetite, sleep, and pain; and 95% of it is produced in the digestive track (Moyer, Nancy 2019)[8].

When you maintain a healthy diet, your body produces "good bacteria," which make up your intestinal microblame. These "good bacteria" help block "bad bacteria," and help you absorb nutrients and they limit inflammation. The more good bacteria in your body, the more serotonin your body produces. However, bad bacteria releases oxidants, toxins, and free radicals that can ultimately damage the brain's cells.

Recent studies reveal the area of the brain most affected by a poor diet is the hippocampus, which controls one's learning, emotions, memory, and the autonomic nervous system.

When one eats nutrient-dense foods like vegetables, fruits, whole grains, and fish rich in Omega 3s, it helps protect the hippocampus (Gomez-Pinilla, 2008)[9]. You can increase the hippocampal genesis with exercise, enriched environments, and caloric restrictions, which decrease oxidative stress that leads to signs of aging and mental decline.

The line between one's diet and one's mental health is not only relegated to adults. In a study conducted by the American Academy of Child and Adolescent Psychiatry published by Elsevier, Inc., researchers found "among mothers and children, early nutritional exposures were independently related to the risk for behavioral and emotional problems in children."

Perhaps your child's clouded thinking and emotional outbursts are directly related to their diet? I can confidently say based on research, their diet could certainly play a part.

Neuro-Nutritional Plan

Developing a "**Neuro-Nutritional Plan**" will help you stay mentally healthy and strong while blissfully traveling down the road of life. With just a few nutritional changes, your body can multiply the "good stuff" your brain needs to repair itself.

With so much at risk, namely everything, changing your diet to include "wise food" is the second step to you being proactive with taking care of your mental health.

Smart Foods (Wise Foods)

The following is a list of foods that are accepted by experts in neuropathology as foods beneficial to the brain's health and function.

Packing your diet with "wise food" will fuel you for the next high-powered business meeting or for your daughter's next volleyball tournament. Nutrients fuel your brain from being overrun by stress.

To fuel your brain, you must protect it with meals that include brightly colored fruits and vegetables, foods that are high in Omega 3s, fatty acids, legumes, nuts, and seeds.

Foods Packed with Brain Power

Berries – Berries have neuroprotective effects that can help guard you from neurodegenerative disease. Below are some additional benefits of berries (Ware, Megan RDN, 2017)[10]:

- Improve communication between brain cells.
- Reduce inflammation throughout the body.
- Increase plasticity, which helps brain cells form new connections, boosting learning and memory.
- Delay age-related neurodegenerative diseases and cognitive decline.

Below are berries that are effective:
- Strawberries
- Blackberries
- Blueberries
- Black currants
- Mulberries

Omega 3s – Omega 3s build cell membranes in the brain as well as reduce symptoms of bipolar disorder. It doesn't stop there Omega 3s also repair brain cells and increase blood flow to the brain, which are links between better cognition and reasoning.

Below are foods that are rich in Omega 3s:
- Mackeral
- Tuna
- Herring
- Sardines
- Wild Salmon

Pillar Two: Nutrition and Mental Health

Nuts and Seeds - Nuts and seeds help with cognitive decline and contain Omega 3s, which protect the brain from oxidative stress caused by free radicals. Free radicals damage cells, proteins and DNA by altering their chemical structure." (Merriam Webster, 1828)11.

Below are some nuts and seeds that help deter coginitive decline:

- Sunflower seeds
- Almonds
- Hazelnuts

Avocados - Avocados contribute to healthy blood flow and could aid in lowering your blood pressure.

Whole Grains - Whole grains can reduce the risk of heart disease by promoting good blood flow to the organ systems.

Below are some whole grains that are beneficial:

- Bulgur wheat
- Whole-grain bread and pasta
- Oatmeal
- Brown rice

Beans- Beans stabilize glucose (blood-sugar levels)
Below is a list of beans that are high in Omega3s

- Edamame
- Kidney beans
- Soy beans

Freshly Brewed Tea/Coffee – Coffee and Tea serve as an antioxidant and in moderation, can help with focus and mood. Some teas and coffees contain caffeine, which is a central nervous system stimulant.

Dark Chocolate – Dark chocolate holds antioxidant properties. "Contains cocoa, also known as cacao. Cacao contains flavonoids, a type of antioxidant that stimulates blood flowing to the brain. It also encourages neuron and blood-vessel growth in parts of the brain involved in memory and learning." (Burgess, Lana 2018)[12]

Lastly, I'd like to also suggest adding the spice tumeric to your diet as some clients have told me it helps with insomnia and raises low mood. (Sass, 2016)[13]

Wise-Food Challenge

Now that you are equipped with the tools you need to ward off brain or engine failure, I want to encourage you to take the "**Wise-Food Challenge**."

For the next two weeks, begin to include "wise foods" into your neuro-nutritional plan. Pay close attention to how you feel, your energy level, and the amount of inflammation in your body.

After two weeks, begin to slowly add your old foods back into your diet and observe how you feel.

Journal the difference in how you felt when you were intentionally eating "wise foods" and when you reintroduced your normal diet into your body.

Then ask yourself: Did your brain function better after the "wise-food" challenge?

Pillar Two: Nutrition and Mental Health

_____

_____

_____

_____

_____

_____

_____

_____

_____

_____

_____

_____

_____

Below are a few recipes to help you get started.

One-Pan Salmon with Roasted Asparagus

Serves 2
Cook: 50 Minutes

8 Asparagus spears - halved
2 Handfuls of cherry tomatoes
1 Tbsp balsamic vinegar
2 Salmon fillets, about 140g
1 handful basil leaves
5 potatoes
1 Tbsp Olive Oil

1. Heat oven to 220C. Put the potatoes and 1 tbsp of olive oil into an ovenproof dish, then roast the potatoes 20 minutes until they start to brown. Toss the asparagus in with the potatoes, then return to the oven for 15 minutes.
2. Throw in the cherry tomatoes and vinegar and nestle the salmon amongst the vegetables. Drizzle with the remaining oil and return to the oven for a final 10 to 15 minutes until the salmon is cooked. Scatter basil leaves over the ingredients. Serve everything scooped straight from the dish, (BBC Good Food, 2008)[14].

Chicken and Avocado Salad with Blueberry Balsamic Dressing

Serves 2
Cook: 40 Minutes

1 garlic clove
85g blueberries
1 tbsp extra virgin olive oil
2 tsp balsamic vinegar
125g fresh or frozen baby broad beans
1 large cooked beetroot, finely chopped
1 avocado, stoned, peeled and sliced
85g bag mixed baby leaf salad

1. Finely chop the garlic. Mash ½ the blueberries with the oil, vinegar and some black pepper in large salad bowl.
2. Boil the broad beans for 5 minutes until just tender. Drain, leaving them unshelled.
3. Stir the garlic into the dressing, and then pile in the warm beans and remaining blueberries with the beetroot, avocado salad and chicken. Toss the mix, but don't go overboard or the juice from the beetroot will turn everything pink.
4. Pile onto plates or into shallow bowls to serve (BBC Good Food, 2008)15.

Pillar 3:
Meditation And Mental Health

Focus your Life in the direction that you want to go and use Meditation to help you.

Meditation and Mental Health

*Focus your Life in the direction that you want to go
and use Meditation to help you.*

Today's fast-paced world has caused many people
to feel overwhelmed, under accomplished, and
frankly, incomplete. When asked, most people
can't fully explain why they feel the way that they
do and most troubling, some even admit to not
seeking help to find out the reason. Instead, a lot
of people feel pressured to embark upon a life
twisting on a carousel of mindless activities and
dictated by a "to-do" list filled with other people's
requests.

This "zombie-like" existence has led to a
disconnect in people from not only themselves
but also to the world around them. One doesn't
have to look hard to find this truth as you can see
people glued to their cell phones instead of
engaging with others standing right next to them.

Pillar Three: Mental Health and Meditation

There is a correlation we can draw between the heightened use of technology and the heightened diagnosis of General Anxiety Disorder and Major Depressive Disorder. I've personally seen an increase of disorders resulting from elevated usage of technology in my private practice. Society has become more disconnected from "true self/gut" than ever before.

However, we must stay connected to our true selves in order to be truly happy and whole. Meditation will help you to do just that.

Meditation – A Journey to a Clear Mind

Meditation is defined in Merriam-Webster's dictionary as "engaging in contemplation or reflection." In practical terms, mediation is clearing your mind and thoughts from all outside distractions. Meditation helps you quiet your mind and focus on your inner voice or what some would call your "gut." You've heard the saying "Listen to your gut because your gut knows the answer." That saying is true but many don't understand what that means or how to hear what their "gut" is saying.

Clients will look at me with a side eye when I ask them, "What is their 'gut,' in this sense of the word, telling them?" Before they begin the work with me, initially their response is usually that of Gary Coleman in the show "Different Strokes" as he would say, "What you talk'n about Willis?" Willis was a character on a well-known sitcom called, Different Strokes in the late 1980s.
So let me take some time to explain it here. Your "gut" in this sense is referring to your inner voice that you were created with. This voice speaks to you as your spirit with messages from whom you believe your creator is (God, Allah, Yahweh, Jehovah, etc.). From this place information is rooted in truth, honesty, love, loyalty, clarity, and security.

For example, my spiritual belief is that God is my Creator and since I was created in His image, my spirit "gut" is how I receive my information straight from Him. Although there are many differences in theological doctrine, one concept is the same. In regards to the three Western religions - Judaism, Christianity, and Sufism of Islam - all assert that we are created in the likeness and image of God.

Furthermore, we were born, yet conceived with the power to co-create our experiences here on Earth through our actions.

However, we cannot do it successfully without staying connected to our Creator for clarity.

We need to stay near and open to hear and feel His messages to us, which can be facilitated by meditation. Meditation keeps your mind clear and your spirit grounded so that you receive the Creator's messages with clarity. You need clarity in order to keep your mind focused so that you make decisions in life that are healthiest for you.

Benefits of Meditation

There are many overall health benefits to meditating, but meditation is essential for brain balance and inner peace. Meditation is he practice of grounding yourself and quieting your mind o that you can block out the outside noise of the world to feel more stable, grounded, and absent of mental boundaries.

Below are the top three widely believed mental-health benefits of meditation.

Meditation's Mental- Health Benefits:

1. **Reduces Stress** - Meditation can reduce your stress by restoring your calm and inner peace. The higher your stress level, the more your body produces a hormone called cortisol. Cortisol's harmful effects disrupt sleep, promote depression

and anxiety, and increases blood pressure and appetite.

2. **Promotes Emotional Health -** According to the National Institute of Health, meditation decreases symptoms of depression.

3. **Controls Anxiety** – Studies reveal meditation can be helpful in controlling paranoid thoughts, obsessive-compulsive behaviors, panic attacks, phobias, and social anxiety (Dr. Thorpe, 2017)[16].

In addition to the top three mental-health benefits of meditation, studies report additional benefits can also include: lengthened attention span, better sleep, enhanced self-awareness, and aid in the fight against addiction.

Forms of Meditation

How you choose to meditate is completely your personal decision. There are many forms of meditation and you have the power to choose which form is right for you.

Because meditation is about you finding inner peace and quiet, below is a list of the most recognized forms of meditation to help you decide.

Breath Awareness meditation, zen meditation, yoga, prayer, kundalini meditation, transcendental meditation, and the type I use personally and prescribe in my private practice, Mindfulness Meditation.

1. Mindfulness refers to a meditation practice that gives special attention to present-moment awareness. The therapeutic uses of Mindfulness has increased over the past 30 years. There is an immense amount of scientific research that supports its health benefits for your mental health. The root reaches back to the teaching of Dr. Jon Kaba-Zinn.

Mindfulness classes have been employed to reduce symptoms of depression, stress and anxiety, and in the treatment of drug addiction. The Mindfulness meditation model has been used at hospitals, schools, prisons and veteran centers.

Breath awareness is a form of mindfulness meditation - The goal of breathing meditation is to focus only on breathing and to ignore other thoughts that enter the mind (Dr. Davis, Dr. Hayes, 2012)[17.] Research has found that mindfulness can:

*   Reduce fixation on negative emotions
*   Improve focus
*   Improve memory
*   Lessen impulsive, emotional reactions
*   Improve relationship satisfaction

2. Kundalini yoga is a physically active form of meditation that blends movements with deep breathing and mantras.

A 2008 study of veterans with chronic low-back pain, for instance, found that yoga reduced pain, increased energy, and improved overall mental health (Villines, Zawn 2017)[18].

3. Transcendental Meditation (TM) is a technique for avoiding distracting thoughts and promoting a state of relaxed awareness. The late Maharishi Mahesh Yogi brought the technique to the United States.

While meditating, the person practices sitting in a comfortable position with their eyes closed and silently repeat a mantra. A mantra is a word or sound used to focus your concentration.

According to the "practitioners," the ordinary thinking process is transcended by a state of pure consciousness.

4. The last style of a well-known form of meditation is prayer. Prayer is defined as a solemn request for help or expression of thanks addressed to God or to an object of worship (Merriam-Webster, 1828)[19].

In conclusion, the form of meditation you choose to do is your own personal choice. The overall goal is to quiet the mind and focus on the "here and now" while connecting to your inner voice. It is beneficial to practice some form of meditation daily so that the stimuli of the world does not distract you from yourself. Being aligned with you is what brings inner peace and joy.

Wise-Meditation Challenge

Over the next week, use the following lines to journal how meditating feels to you. Try to name three aspects you liked about meditating, and also list one thing you found challenging about meditating.

_____

_____

_____

_____

_____

_____

_____

Pillar Three: Meditation and Mental Health

Pillar 4:

Sleep and Mental Health

When you quiet your mind, you will find your answers.

Sleep and Mental Health

When you quiet your mind, you will find your answers.

Creating the life you desire takes a lot of physical and mental energy, and it all begins with how well you sleep. Sleep is necessary to keep your brain functioning well. Loss of sleep causes delirium, confusion, and delay in the ability to process information. You must shut your brain down by sleeping because it needs regular maintenance and repair.

When you're asleep your brain and body regenerates what was damaged the day before. Sleep gives your brain time to refresh at 100 percent so when you're awake and need to rely on it, it will work at its best.

When you're asleep you give your neurotransmitters time to rejuvenate in order to connect optimally.

Beyond its restorative benefits to the body, sleep is integral to how your brain performs; moreover, sleep is necessary to keep your brain functioning cognitively. Loss of sleep causes delirium, confusion and delay in the ability to process information. Despite this fact, according to the Centers of Disease Control (CDC), 50 to 70 million Americans suffer from ongoing chronic sleep disorders (Centers of Disease Control and Prevention, 2017)[20].

With 70 different types of recognized sleep disorders, Pillar 3, "Sleep and Mental Health," is critical to understanding how and why you don't get the rejuvenating rest you need, and most importantly how to create an environment that will help you fall and stay fast asleep (Dr. Swierzewski, III, 2016)[21].

Types of Sleeping Disorders
The most familiar types of sleep disorders include:

Insomnia – Insomnia is as a "sleep disorder that is characterized by difficulty falling and/or staying asleep," according to Merriam-Webster's online dictionary.

For those of you who are experiencing insomnia and have decided to use melatonin supplements regularly, I'm encouraging you to rethink that decision and here's why. According to a survey by the National Center for Complimentary and Integrative Health, melatonin can benefit people whose internal clock doesn't line up with their location, such as those experiencing jet lag; however it's not a sleep aid.

Melatonin is naturally released by the body when the sun goes down, setting off a series of events that ready you for sleep. "If you take it at inconsistent times, you're convincing your body that you're constantly moving time zones" (Edlund, Matthew 2019)[22].

In addition, The American College of Physicians recommends Cognitive Behavior Therapy, behavioral interventions like sleep restriction therapy, and stimulus control to treat insomnia, not melatonin.

Obstructive Sleep Apnea – Obstructive Sleep Apnea occurs when your throat muscles intermittently relax and block your airway during sleep. Snoring is an indication that you may have this very common sleep disorder.

Various Movement Syndromes – Various movement syndromes include a sleep disorder that causes sensations through your body that lead to night fidgeting.

Narcolepsy – Narcolepsy is defined as "a sleep disorder characterized by excessive sleepiness, sleep paralysis, hallucinations, and in some cases episodes of cataplexy (partial or total loss of muscle control, often triggered by a strong emotion such as laughter)" according to Webster's online dictionary.

As indicated, millions of people struggle to get the rest they need to lead a productive life. For many, though they are lying in bed, they still find it hard to rest peacefully throughout the night.

The reason or the "why" varies from person to person. People point to busy schedules, health problems, and a myriad of other reasons as to why they are unable to rest properly. Add stimuli from a glaring TV or the light from a cell phone, and one soon finds themselves hitting the alarm clock only after being in a deep sleep, (called REM sleep) for one or two hours.

According to an article published by the US National Library of Medicine Institute of Health, "Short sleep can negatively impact some aspects of the brain's function to a similar degree as alcohol intoxication"(Leech MS, 2018)23.

So, if you've ever felt a bit tipsy but have not had anything to drink, it may be because you have not gotten enough deep sleep for a long enough period of time throughout the sleep cycle.

Sleep Cycles

When you are tired, this is due to the amount of energy and brain power that you used during the day, go to sleep. Your circadian rhythm is also responsible for you feeling sleepy. The rhythm is a 24-hour internal clock that is running in the background of your brain. It cycles between sleepiness and alertness at regular intervals. It's also known as your sleep/wake cycle. The hypothalamus controls your circadian rhythm.

There are four stages of sleep that rotate in a cycle throughout the night. Your body operates on a 24-hour internal clock called the circadian rhythm. A complete sleep cycle takes an average of 90 to 110 minutes with each stage lasting between 5 to 15 minutes.

Stage 1 – Light stage of sleep
Stage 2 – Deeper sleep / less able to be awakened
Stage 3 – Progressively deeper sleep also called
            SWS – slow-wave sleep or delta sleep
Stage 4 - REM Sleep – Deep Sleep

How Much Sleep is Enough?

There is an appropriate amount of sleep that we should get determined by our age. I'll start by giving you the amount of sleep that children need then continue to provide you with the amount of sleep needed through adulthood.

Children

A 2-year-old child requires about 14 hours of sleep each night, and a 9-year-old as much as 12 hours of sleep; however, an adult who is middle-aged only requires about eight hours to function well.

Inadequate sleep during early childhood affects brain development and the manner in which children socialize.

Teens

The teenage brain is in a process of development. According to a 2018 study, "High schoolers who slept less than six hours a night were twice as likely to use alcohol, tobacco, or marijuana as those who slept eight hours, and were three times as likely to consider or attempt suicide" (Mozes, 2018)[24].

Teenagers need sleep, so please stop waking them up because "you" are awake and you believe that they should be awake too. Lack of sleep can result in a greater chance of fascination in risky behavior due to the effects felt in the pre-frontal cortex of the brain and the amygdale (National Sleep Foundation, 2019)25.

"There's a big growth spurt in adolescents when about one-third of the neuroconnections in the brain die and reorganize in a rather radical way, which requires more sleep,"(Matthew Edlund)22.

Adults
Adults 25 to middle age need seven to nine hours of sleep each night for optimal mental functioning. Even people over the age of 65 need at least seven to eight hours of sleep a night, however it's understood due to other physical challenges and changes in lifestyle they may get less.

NOTE: "The leading threats to sleep later in life are psychiatric illnesses, physical illnesses, and the side effects from some medications used to treat them (National Sleep Foundation, 2019)26. If this is a problem for you, please seek treatment from a health-care professional because you need to get the appropriate amount of sleep recommended."

Setting the Mood for Sleep
Choose to take care of your mind by preparing for your brain's regeneration during sleep. This is big! You must learn how to take care of you.

1. **Turn all of the lights off** in your room so that the room is dark. Turn off the television and other electronics like your phone and computer which stimulate your brain to stay awake and focus. When your brain recognizes any type of light, even when your eyes are closed, it wants to rev up and prepare to work. Give your brain rest, shut everything off.

2. **Turn the temperature in the room down,** studies show that we get a better quality of rest when the room is dark and cool. You can also add a sound machine if you feel as though your mind can't shut down because of the noises that are recognized in the room.

3. **Don't do anything that will stimulate your brain** before you fall asleep. Shutting down for the evening should include detoxing your mind from all negative thoughts before you fall asleep.

There is research that supports using a weighted blanket to ensure a good night's sleep. A 2015 study found that weighted blankets helped individuals to settle down to sleep more easily and to sleep longer (Doheny, Kathleen)27.

Over the years in my private practice many people who report having difficulty sleeping also report feeling high levels of anxiety. I'm told that they fear "never" going to sleep and how not sleeping is going to ruin their day. Some even have an irrational fear that not sleeping could ruin their life.

I teach them how to let that irrational thought go and accept the fact that sleep sometimes varies from night to night in response to the events of the day and the amount of stimuli exposed to the brain.

Clients have told me the fear of forgetting something they are thinking about has hindered them from falling asleep.

If you notice that there are thoughts in your mind that are racing because you are fearful that you may forget them, write them down on paper. Then you can choose to let the fear of forgetting the information goes so you can get some sleep. I encourage my clients to keep a pen and paper in their nightstand by their bed for times like these.

Wise-Sleep Challenge

I challenge you to get six to eight hours of sleep per night for one week. Use the following lines to journal how your brain has benefited from getting more sleep.

_____

_____

_____

_____

_____

_____

_____

_____

_____

_____

_____

_____

_____

Pillar 5:
Learning New Things and Mental Health

Take care of your mind if you want your mind to take care of you!

Learning New Things and Mental Health

Take care of your mind if you want your mind to take care of you!

It is healthiest to be a lifelong learner, Pillar 5, Learning New Things and Mental Health will teach you how. Merriam-Webster's online dictionary defines learning as gaining knowledge, developing skills and having new experiences that enrich your life. Don't we all want an enriched life?

What's so amazing about your brain is it never gets too old to learn something new. As you get older, your brain has the ability to learn and grow through a process called brain neuroplasticity.

Neuroplasticity is the ability of the brain to change continuously throughout an individual's lifetime. Changes include: pruning, deleting, moving, and renewing. I'm hoping that you knowing your brain has the ability to learn new things throughout your lifespan is empowering and encourages your commitment to keep learning.

This commitment can delay the degenerative effects to the brain by improving memory and intelligence while decreasing anxiety and stabilizing your mood.

In an article in the Harvard Medical School Journal, the author noted, embracing a new activity that forces you to think, learn and requires ongoing practice, can be one of the best ways to keep your brain healthy (Harvard Medical School, 2019)[28].

THE BRAIN AND LEARNING

Your brain's learning power increases as the white matter or the myelin becomes denser. Myelin, which gives gray matter its color, helps improve performance on a number of tasks the more you practice. I teach my clients to learn something new, then to practice, practice, practice!

Learning new skills stimulate neurons in the brain, which form more neural pathways and allow electrical impulses to travel faster across them.

SECONDARY BENEFITS OF LEARNING NEW THINGS

1. **Increases your self esteem**
   When you learn something new, you experience a feeling of accomplishment, which makes you feel better about yourself. Feeling a sense of accomplishment raises the level of dopamine in your brain so you get a boost of natural "feel good."

2. **Encourages more social interactions**
   Being committed to learning new things may have you in a new dance class, book club, cooking class and/or sewing class interacting with new people. It's healthy to have others to connect with to avoid isolation.
   Isolation is not good for anyone. Connect to the world around you while learning something that you never thought you could do.

3. **Improves Cognitive Functioning**
   Cognitive functioning includes, but is not limited to, your ability to reason, problem-solve and memorize, which all require brain power. Creative outlets like painting, learning an instrument or even a new language, are all ways to improve your cognitive functioning.

4. Helps ward off dementia
Engaging in mentally stimulating activities can strengthen your brain's power at any age (Harvard Medical School, 2017)[29].

According to alz.org the term "dementia" describes a group of symptoms associated with a decline in memory or other thinking skills severe enough to reduce a person's ability to perform everyday activities.

ACTIVITIES THAT IMPROVE YOUR BRAIN'S POWER

In order for your learning activities to be beneficial, according to Dr. John N. Norris, director of social and health policy research at the Harvard-affiliated Institute for Aging Research, states, "Embracing a new activity that also forces you to think and learn and requires ongoing practice can be one of the best ways to keep the brain healthy" (Norris 2019)[30].

Make sure that what you choose to learn includes the following:

1. Challenging
Pick a craft, hobby or learning experience that challenges you to learn something which expands or betters your skill set. If you can't swim, try it. If you have always dreamed of playing the piano, it is never too late.

2. Complexity

When you learn something that is complex, you engage your brain in critical thinking and problem solving. Activities like quilting and digital photography helped improve the memory of elderly patients between 60 to 90 years of age (Dr. Park 2013)[31].

3. Practice

Practicing a new skill helps you get better at it. Repetition not only helps improve your memory, but it also helps you to develop your skills.

Below I've listed some powerful brain-building activities that are beneficial to powering up your brain and protecting your mental health.

- **Play games that stimulate your mind**
  Research varies but it all agrees on one thing, stimulating your mind through games is beneficial to your brain's continual development.
  - Picture Puzzles
  - Strategy Games
  - Crossword Puzzles
  - Visualization Puzzles
  - Card Games
  - Computer Games

- **Writing**
  Writing stimulates your brain, requires concentration and challenges you to express your thoughts and feelings.

Below are some easy ways you can integrate writing into your learning process.
- Poems
- Articles
- Book
- Journal Daily

- **Create Something New**
  Being creative challenges you to think critically and engages the creative side (right) of your brain. Below are some suggestions on how you can be more creative and enhance your mental well-being.
- Painting on a canvas or your bedroom walls.
- Planting or creating a floral arrangement.
- Rearranging the furniture in your space/redecorating.
- Creating a scrapbook.

There are so many challenging yet fun things you can do to guard your mental health. When I began, I mentioned the only thing that can stop you from learning is your commitment to it.

The Wise-Learning Challenge

Decide today to make learning something new a
focal point of your life in the **"Wise-Learning
Challenge."** Use the following lines to journal
about what you decided to learn and how your
brain has improved as a result of it.

_____

_____

_____

_____

_____

_____

_____

_____

_____

_____

_____

_____

_____

_____

_____

_____

_____

_____

_____

_____

_____

_____

_____

_____

Pillar 6: Psychotherapy and Mental Health

The smartest person in the room is not the one who is most intelligent, but the one who recognizes what they want and does whatever they need to do to go get it!

Psychotherapy and Mental Health

The smartest person in the room is not the one who is most intelligent, but the one who recognizes what they want and does whatever they need to do to go get it!

The stigma associated with the subject of mental health has made it a taboo topic in many communities. Sadly this stigma attaches a mark of shame, disgrace and dishonor to it. Unfortunately the general public does not know the difference between mental health and mental illness, thus some may see mental illness as a weakness without understanding the complexities of the brain and genetics.

The truth is, if you are experiencing high levels of anxiety, feeling unmotivated and stuck or believe you are suffering from signs of depression or PTSD, talking to a mental health professional is the most empowering thing you can do.

Pillar Six: Psychotherapy and Mental Health

There is a difference between mental health and mental illness. Mental illness refers to a wide range of mental disorders that affect your mood, thinking, and behavior while mental health includes psychological, emotional and social well-being.

Mental health determines how we handle stress, relate to others and make choices that affect our quality of life. Mental illness does not discriminate; anyone can be affected by it, regardless of your age, gender, socioeconomic class, race, ethnicity, religion, culture, or finances.

Moreover, research supports that there is a genetic predisposition to mental illness. Having a genetic predisposition does not mean that you will become mentally ill; however, just like with the predisposition for illnesses such as diabetes, high cholesterol, or heart disease, you have to work harder than others to prevent it (Hyman, 2000)[32]. In addition, brain chemistry: and life experiences such as trauma and abuse contribute to mental decline, which is treatable.

The daily pressures of life can be overwhelming for anyone, especially when you don't possess the coping skills that can protect you from mental burnout!

Throughout this book, I have given you a powerpack in the form of six pillars that will help you protect your mental health. This final pillar will help you to recognize the importance of seeking help when you need it. Let's begin with discussing the reason you may be experiencing some difficulties.

NUEROTRANSMITTERS

So now let me introduce you to the "WHY." There are reasons "why" you may be experiencing a low level of motivation or energy, high anxiety, irregular moods, irritability, inability to concentrate, racing thoughts, confusion, sadness, anger and/or depression.

Your brain has neurons and neurotransmitters that govern the way you process information, perceive circumstances, feel and make decisions. Neurotransmitters help to regulate mental performance, emotional states, physical energy, and pain response.

They are mainly in the central nervous system and are active anywhere there are nerves, such as your stomach and muscles. If you find yourself having issues with any of the latter, you should continue to read on to learn how to create change in your thinking.

Here is a list with a short description of the major neurotransmitters defined (Dr. Maiese, 2019)33. The list is broken down and explained well.

Dopamine is a 'focus' neurotransmitter that regulates motor behavior, motivation, pleasure, and emotional arousal. Elevated dopamine levels have been associated with schizophrenia, while low levels can be associated with addiction, cravings, certain forms of depression, and the muscular rigidity and tremors found in Parkinson's disease.

Epinephrine (adrenaline) is involved in energy and glucose metabolism. Low levels of epinephrine are associated with depression.

Norepinephrine (noradrenaline) is used in the "flight-or-flight" response.

GABA (gamma-Aminobutyric acid) inhibits anxiety and stress. Too little GABA is associated with anxiety and anxiety disorders. Some antidepressants can increase levels of GABA at the receptor sites.

Endorphins are affiliated with feelings of euphoria, and reduce perception of pain in the body. Increased levels of physical activity such as exercise cause a release of endorphins. This may help to alleviate symptoms of depression.

Serotonin influences mood, sleep, and appetite (including carbohydrate cravings), and plays a role in impulsive and aggressive behavior. Too little serotonin is associated with depression and some anxiety disorders such as obsessive-compulsive disorder (OCD).

Acetylcholine is involved in voluntary movement, learning, memory, and sleep. Low levels of acetylcholine are associated with the symptoms of depression, while low levels in the hippocampus (a part of the brain linked to memory) have been associated with dementia.

There are several different diagnoses of mental illness. Mental illnesses are diagnosed due to the symptoms that are being experienced by the person and determined by the criteria in the DSM-5. The most common are: Depression, Anxiety, Post-Traumatic Stress Disorder (PTSD), ADHD/ADD, Bipolar Disorder and Schizophrenia.

TYPES OF THERAPY

The brain has well over 100 billion neurons and neurotransmitters; however, the amount and how they interact is different in everyone's body. Some people have deficiencies in specific neurotransmitters due to genetics or medical reasons. Sometimes pharmaceutical treatment is necessary to inhibit or assist neurotransmitters in the brain.

If you have applied these six pillars and continue to have psychological and physical symptoms that impede your functioning, seek professional help from a psychiatrist, psychotherapist, psychologist and/or a primary-care physician for a medical and psychological assessment.

Remember to continue to work these six pillars of mental health with or without pharmaceutical treatment so that your brain will work at its best. Mental-health professionals specialize in different areas. My area of expertise is as a psychotherapist.

As a psychotherapist, my goal is to help people break dysfunctional cycles, face challenges, and overcome barriers in order to live the quality of life they desire. I provide individual, couples, and family counseling using research-based therapy approaches for adolescents, adults, and families.

I utilize a non-judgmental approach to therapy. My method of practice is contingent upon each individual and centered on that person's need.

The goal of therapy is to help each person find healthy solutions to lead full and productive lives as they see it.

I'm intentional about creating an environment in which my clients feel comfortable and safe to explore their innermost thoughts, needs and emotions. I believe in "peeling" back the layers of life and helping clients get to the root of their issues.

One form of treatment that I use to help clients change behavior is Cognitive Behavioral Therapy (CBT). CBT is a form of psychological treatment that has been demonstrated to be effective for a range of problems including depression, anxiety disorders, alcohol and drug-use problems, marital problems, eating disorders and severe mental illness. Numerous research studies suggest that CBT leads to significant improvement in functioning and quality of life. In many studies, CBT has been demonstrated to be as effective as, or more effective than, other forms of psychological therapy or psychiatric medications (Society of Clinical Psychology)[34].

Ultimately, CBT challenges a client's distorted cognitions to change destructive patterns of behavior.

Seeking Help

As mentioned earlier in the chapter, seeking help is a brave act on your part to protect your mental health and ultimately, your life. One of the most important things you can do is to learn to recognize when your brain is malfunctioning and/or when it is time to get help.

As a psychotherapist with years of experience in the field, I've witnessed many people who others assume "should" be mentally healthy yet after a traumatic event experience a mental illness. I am passionate about teaching and empowering others to make mental health a part of their everyday lifestyle.

Symptoms for mental illness vary from extreme paranoia to mild depression; however, if you don't know how to recognize when you are struggling mentally, small mental-health issues can balloon into major problems that disrupt your life (Dr. Lieber, 2019)[35]. Below I have provided some symptoms from the DSM -5 (Diagnostic and Statistical Manual of Mental Disorders, 5th Edition: DSM-5)[36] that may be a cause of concern and a message that you need to seek help.

Signs of Major Depressive Disorder

- Feelings of sadness, tearfulness, emptiness or hopelessness
- Angry outbursts, irritability or frustration over small matters
- Loss of interest or pleasure in most or all normal activities, such as sex, hobbies or sports

- Sleep disturbances, including insomnia or sleeping too much
- Tiredness and lack of energy
- Reduced appetite and weight loss or increased cravings for food and weight gain
- Anxiety, agitation, or restlessness
- Slowed thinking, speaking, or body movements
- Feelings of worthlessness or guilt, fixating on past failures, or self-blame
- Trouble thinking, concentrating, making decisions, and remembering things
- Frequent or recurrent thoughts of death, suicidal thoughts, suicide attempts, or suicide
- Unexplained physical problems, such as back pain or headaches

Signs of General Anxiety Disorder

- Excessive, ongoing worry and tension
- An unrealistic view of problems
- Restlessness or a feeling of being "edgy"
- Irritability
- Muscle tension
- Headaches
- Sweating
- Difficulty concentrating
- Nausea
- The need to go to the bathroom frequently
- Tiredness

Pillar Six: Psychotherapy and Mental Health

- Trouble falling or staying asleep
- Trembling
- Being easily startled

Below are some mental-health resources.

National Suicide Prevention Lifeline: 1-800-273-8255

SAMHSA Treatment Referral Helpline: 1-877-726-4727

Family NAMI Helpline: 800-950-6264
info@nami.org

"Psychology Today" www.psychologytoday.com

The National Domestic Violence Hotline: 800-799-7233

Anxiety and Depression Association of America (ADAA): 240-485-1001

Children and Adults with Attention-Deficit/Hyperactivity Disorder (CHADD): 800-233-4050

Depression and Bipolar Support Alliance (DBSA): 800-826-3632

PSYCHOTHERAPY (THERAPY) PAYMENT OPTIONS

Those of you who think you cannot afford therapy may be wrong. There are many options on how to pay for therapy. Depending on where you live will determine the price of therapy in your area.

The price of a 50-minute session can range from $80 to $300. Another option is using your behavioral health benefits through your medical-insurance plan. In addition, sometimes your employer may offer a specific number of free sessions paid for by what is called an "Employee Assistance Program" (EAP). Check with your Human Resource department to find out what your EAP benefits are.

Some therapists have a private practice and will slide their payment scale to a lower rate determined by what is fair to them and what the client can afford.

If you are not opposed to "group" therapy, it is usually less expensive than individual and couples therapy. Last but not least, you may qualify for therapy that is free provided by community agencies. There are many ways to go about paying for therapy, don't give up on getting the help that you need, there is affordable help available.

As we close, decide today to commit to being proactive with taking care of your mind. Remember, your mind is your body's engine and you need it to operate at its best in order to get you where you want to go.

Your mind affects your finances, career, romantic relationships, familial relationships, friendships and parenting.

A healthy mind "mental health" will lead you to the quality of life you desire.

Mental Health is a Lifestyle! ®

WISE-HELP CHALLENGE

Use the following lines to journal about how you imagine it might feel to talk to a trained mental - health professional who is unbiased and eager to help you.

Remember, they want to hear your story and help you create the change that you desire.

_____

_____

_____

Pillar Six: Psychotherapy and Mental Health

About Andrea Wise-Brown

With appearances on "Unfaithful" -- Stories of Betrayal -- on OWN (Oprah Winfrey Network), FOX4 NEWS, SiriusXM, Tom Joyner Morning Show, as well as other media outlets, Andrea Wise-Brown is a leading mental-health expert.

Her mission is to eradicate stigma surrounding mental illness and encourage everyone to make mental health a lifestyle. Andrea is a native of New Jersey where she earned her degree in Psychology/Psychiatric Rehabilitation at University of Medicine and Dentistry of New Jersey/Kean University.

As a Psychotherapist who currently resides in Texas where she earned her M.Ed. in Counseling at the University of North Texas, Andrea is a member of Psi Chi and Texas Counseling Association. She is a Licensed Professional Counselor, a National Certified Counselor, and has been formerly trained as a Hostage Negotiator.

Andrea's compassionate approach helps families, individuals and couples while using research-based therapy that is centered on the person's need. By creating an environment in which her clients feel comfortable and safe to explore their innermost thoughts, needs and emotions, Andrea helps adolescents, families and adults find healthy solutions to the productive lives they want to see.

About Andrea Wise-Brown

From college and business seminars, to team building and women's retreats, Andrea specializes in providing strategies and skill training to overcome life's barriers.

Her clinical experiences include but are not limited to treating anxiety, eating disorders, behavioral issues, depression, loss or grief, family of origin trauma and anger-management. Andrea is passionate about empowering everyone to power-up their brain so that they can live the life that they desire!

Acknowledgements

First and foremost, I would like to thank God for breath, passion and the resilience to serve my Life's purpose!

To my mother, Lorraine "Big Red," who has always been there to empower me to dream big and achieve even bigger. I get my strength from you. My sister Darlene, silent yet strong and loyal, Mr. Tom, kind and nurturing, I'm grateful.

To my husband, Tariq "KB," thank you for always supporting my dreams and aspirations. You ride with me even when the road is unclear. Thanks for always fighting for me.

My daughter, Ayanna, thank you for always being your authentic beautiful self. You are intellectually and emotionally brilliant beyond your years; your advice and accomplishments never cease to amaze me. I'm elated that God shared you with me!

My Sons: Sahaad, our spiritual connection is like no other, it's magical. Jamal, I excitedly looked forward to your arrival before you entered this world and my heart continues to dance in your presence. Mekhi, we are soulmates, purposely tied together. You all make my spirit twirl and smile; I could not have asked for better sons.

Auntie Marion, who has been my voice of reason during and beyond my developmental years. Thank you for your love, guidance and unconditional support!

Acknowledgements

Verleen and Murray, who I can always rely on through every transition in my family's life. Thank you for always being a rock for me and my family. Verleen, Zylphia, and Edna, my "OLG" forever and always.

Lewis, Blonnie, Debbie, and Sharon thank you for providing me with a positive image of family. You always made me feel safe, loved and important.

To my Sister Cousins; Toni, Sana, Lateefah, and Zakiyyah. To my cousins; Husain, Toya, Rasheed, Antoine, Makilia, Tiaja, Jamir, Syreeta, Carissa, Sandra, Terry, Peaches, Gail and Jackie. To my nieces and nephews; Malik, Nasir, Ibn, Zia, Brianna, Imani, Ahnyah, Madison, Payton, Kaia, Jahaad, Mekhi and Zoe, I love you all.

To my spirit animal Aunt Vivian, my ride or die Aunt Bessie, the first one who gave me a shot, Aunt Grace and to the one who invited me to stay forever, Aunt Shakirah; Thank you all for being the wind beneath my wings.

To my brother and sisters, Jamar, Hakika and Anthea, thank you for always supporting and loving me. I'm grateful to have you in my life. Scarlett, Sage and my namesake, Samara Andrea Wise, you are destined to accomplish great things and I'm here to support it all!

Acknowledgements

To the Ladies of "Drea's Unique Image," thank you for your loyalty and support! You know who you are, you ladies are my family!

My friends, Tabatha, Celeste, Nikki, Jaqui, Annette, Antoinette, Shawnette, Tanisha, Kelly, Janie, Mehwish, and Katrina; you know how we do. You pull me up and never let me drown.

Angela, my COO, thank you for all that you do. I don't know what I would do without you! I also would like to extend a big thank you to Sara my office manager and Trenette. "I'm grateful to have you in my life."

References

1. Walden University, Dr. Shawan Charles, PhD in Psychology Walden University.
   https://www.waldenu.edu/online-bachelors-programs/bs-in-psychology/resource/five-mental-benefits-of-exercise.

2. National Institute Mental Health
   https://www.nimh.nih.gov/health/statistics/mental-illness.shtml.

3. "Physical Activity Reduces Stress." *Anxiety and Depression Association of America, ADAA*, adaa.org/understanding-anxiety/related-illnesses/other-related-conditions/stress/physical-activity-reduces-st.

4. Godman, Heidi. "Regular Exercise Changes the Brain to Improve Memory, Thinking Skills." *Harvard Health Blog*, 5 Apr. 2018, www.health.harvard.edu/blog/regular-exercise-changes-brain-improve-memory-thinking-skills-201404097110.

5. Dregni, Michael, et al. "This Is Your Brain on Exercise." *Experience Life*, 26 Feb. 2019, experiencelife.com/article/this-is-your-brain-on-exercise/.

6. Sharma, Ashish, et al. "Exercise for Mental Health." *Primary Care Companion to the Journal of Clinical Psychiatry*, Physicians Postgraduate Press, Inc., 2006, www.ncbi.nlm.nih.gov/pmc/articles/PMC1470658/.

References

7. "Omega-3 Fatty Acids: An Essential Contribution."
    The Nutrition Source, 22 May 2019,
    www.hsph.harvard.edu/nutritionsource/what-
    should-you-eat/fats-and-cholesterol/types-of-
    fat/omega-3-fats/.

8. Moyer, Nancy L. "Serotonin Deficiency: Symptoms,
    Causes, Tests & Treatments." *Healthline*,
    Healthline Media, 27 Feb. 2019,
    www.healthline.com/health/serotonin-deficiency.

9. Gómez-Pinilla, Fernando. "Brain Foods: the Effects
    of Nutrients on Brain Function." *Nature
    Reviews. Neuroscience*, U.S. National Library of
    Medicine, July 2008,
    www.ncbi.nlm.nih.gov/pmc/articles/PMC280570
    6/.

10. LD, Megan Ware RDN. "Blueberries: Health
    Benefits, Facts, and Research." *Medical News
    Today*, MediLexicon International, 5 Sept. 2017,
    www.medicalnewstoday.com/articles/287710.ph
    p.

11. "Free Radical." *Merriam-Webster*, Merriam-
    Webster, www.merriam-
    webster.com/dictionary/free%20radical.

12. Burgess, Lana. "12 Best Brain Foods: Memory,
    Concentration, and Brain Health." *Medical News
    Today*, MediLexicon International,
    www.medicalnewstoday.com/articles/324044.ph
    p.

References

13. "You Should Probably Be Eating More Turmeric. Here's How." *Health.com*, www.health.com/nutrition/tumeric-tips.

14. Desmazery, Barney. "One-Pan Salmon with Roast Asparagus." *BBC Good Food*, 1 May 2008, www.bbcgoodfood.com/recipes/5925/onepan-salmon-with-roast-asparagus.

15. Buenfeld, Sara. "Chicken & Avocado Salad with Blueberry Balsamic Dressing." *BBC Good Food*, 1 June 2015, www.bbcgoodfood.com/recipes/chicken-avocado-salad-blueberry-balsamic-dressing.

16. "12 Science-Based Benefits of Meditation." *Healthline*, Healthline Media, www.healthline.com/nutrition/12-benefits-of-meditation.

17. *Monitor on Psychology*, American Psychological Association, www.apa.org/monitor/2012/07-08/ce-corner.

18. Villines, Zawn. "7 Types of Meditation: What Type Is Best for You?" *Medical News Today*, MediLexicon International, www.medicalnewstoday.com/articles/320392.php.

19. "Prayer." *Merriam-Webster*, Merriam-Webster, www.merriam-webster.com/dictionary/prayer.

References

20. "CDC - Data and Statistics - Sleep and Sleep Disorders." *Centers for Disease Control and Prevention*, Centers for Disease Control and Prevention, www.cdc.gov/sleep/data_statistics.html.

21. "Sleep Disorder Overview." *Sleep Disorder Overview - Sleep Disorders - HealthCommunities.com*, www.healthcommunities.com/sleep-disorders/overview-of-sleep-disorders.shtml.

22. "The New Science of Sleep." *Psychology Today*, Sussex Publishers, www.psychologytoday.com/intl/articles/201905/the-new-science-sleep?collection=1107226.

23. "10 Reasons Why Good Sleep Is Important." *Healthline*, Healthline Media, www.healthline.com/nutrition/10-reasons-why-good-sleep-is-important.

24. Mozes, Alan. "Sleepy Teens More Prone to Drug Use, Suicide Attempts." *WebMD*, WebMD, 1 Oct. 2018, www.webmd.com/parenting/news/20181001/sleep-deprived-teens-more-prone-to-risky-behaviors#1.

25. "Sleep for Teenagers." *National Sleep Foundation*, www.sleepfoundation.org/articles/teens-and-sleep.

References

26. "What Causes Insomnia?" *National Sleep Foundation*, www.sleepfoundation.org/insomnia/what-causes-insomnia.

27. Doheny, Kathleen. "Seeking Better Sleep Under a Weighted Blanket." *WebMD*, WebMD, 2 Apr. 2018, www.webmd.com/sleep-disorders/news/20180402/seeking-better-sleep-under-a-weighted-blanket.

28. Harvard Health Publishing. "Train Your Brain." *Harvard Health*, www.health.harvard.edu/mind-and-mood/train-your-brain.

29. Harvard Health Publishing. "6 Simple Steps to Keep Your Mind Sharp at Any Age." *Harvard Health*, www.health.harvard.edu/mind-and-mood/6-simple-steps-to-keep-your-mind-sharp-at-any-age.

30. "Train Your Brain For Building and Maintaining Cognitive Skills." *Vitality Now*, www.vitalitynow.org/articles/train-your-brain.

31. "Thursday, August 1, 2019." *Mentally Challenging Activities Improve Memory as Baby Boomers Age - News Center - The University of Texas at Dallas*, www.utdallas.edu/news/2013/10/22-26961_Mentally-Challenging-Activities-Improve-Memory-as-_story-wide.html.

References

32. Hyman, Steven. *The Genetics of Mental Illness: Implications for Practice*. 2019, www.who.int/bulletin/archives/78(4)455.pdf.

33. "Neurotransmission - Neurologic Disorders." *Merck Manuals Professional Edition*, Merck Manuals, www.merckmanuals.com/professional/neurologic-disorders/neurotransmission/neurotransmission.

34. *What Is Cognitive Behavioral Therapy?* 2019, www.apa.org/ptsd-guideline/patients-and-families/cognitive-behavioral.pdf.

35. "What Is Major Depression? The Signs, Symptoms & Treatment." *Psycom.net - Mental Health Treatment Resource Since 1986*, www.psycom.net/depression.central.major.html.

36. Diagnostic and Statistical Manual of Mental Disorders, 5th Edition: DSM-5.